First & Goal

By Dan Marino

with Greg Brown

Illustrations by Christopher Paluso

TAYLOR PUBLISHING
DALLAS, TEXAS

Greg Brown has been involved in sports for thirty years as an athlete and award-winning sportswriter. Brown started his Positively For Kids series after being unable to find sports books for his own children that taught life lessons. He is the co-author of *Mo Vaughn: Follow Your Dreams; Sheryl Swoopes: Bounce Back; Steve Young: Forever Young; Bonnie Blair: A Winning Edge; Cal Ripken: Count Me In; Troy Aikman: Things Change; Kirby Puckett: Be the Best You Can Be;* and *Edgar Martinez: Patience Pays*. Brown regularly speaks at schools and can be reached at greg@PositivelyForKids.com. He lives in Bothell, Washington, with his wife, Stacy, and two children.

Christopher Paluso's sports illustrations have appeared on numerous magazine covers, plates, and prints. For five years, he provided the cover illustrations for *Legends Sports Memorabilia*, a leading sports collectibles magazine. Many of his plates, prints, and magazine covers have increased significantly in value over the years. Paluso is official artist for the San Diego Hall of Champions Sports Museum (he has painted all eighty-two members of the Hall of Fame) and the San Diego Holiday Bowl Hall of Fame.

All photos courtesy of Dan Marino family unless otherwise noted.

Published by Taylor Publishing Company
1550 West Mockingbird Lane
Dallas, Texas 75235

Designed by Steve Willgren

Library of Congress Cataloging-in-Publication Data

Marino, Dan, 1961–
    First and goal / by Dan Marino with Greg Brown.
        p. cm.
    Summary: The quarterback for the Miami Dolphins describes his childhood in Pittsburgh, his successes and failures in high school and college sports, and his record-breaking career in professional football.
     ISBN 0-87833-958-2
     1. Marino, Dan, 1961– —Juvenile literature. 2. Football players—United States—Biography—Juvenile literature.
3. Miami Dolphins (Football team)—Juvenile literature. [1. Marino, Dan, 1961– . 2. Football players.] I. Brown, Greg. II. Title.
GV939.M29M25 1997
796.332'092—dc21
[B]
                        96-30008
                        CIP
                        AC

Printed in the United States of America

10 9 8 7 6 5 4 3

Dan Marino has donated royalties from the sales of this book to the Dan Marino Foundation, which supports various South Florida children's charities.

Hi! I'm Dan Marino, and I've written this book to share with you some of what I've learned by playing quarterback from the streets of Pittsburgh to the stadiums of the National Football League. My dad used to write me letters to inspire and guide me during my younger days. Think of this book as my letter of encouragement to you.

Most people know my name because I have played for the Miami Dolphins since 1983. From my first experience on a football team as a water boy to playing in a Super Bowl, I've had my share of ups and downs. Playing so long in the NFL, under great coaches and with talented teammates, has helped me set 25 NFL passing records.

I'm proud of those records, but I'm still searching for my dream of winning a Super Bowl.

Throwing the football has given me many riches, and not just money. My experiences in sports—the victories and defeats, joys and pains—have made me a better person off the field. Still, the fame and my successes have not changed me, and I'm as proud of that as my football records.

I'm still the same Danny who grew up in the city row houses, the son of a wise newspaper truck driver who taught me to respect everyone the same.

No, I have not forgotten where I'm from, Western Pennsylvania, an area that has produced the greatest quarterbacks ever. I still can close my eyes and remember.

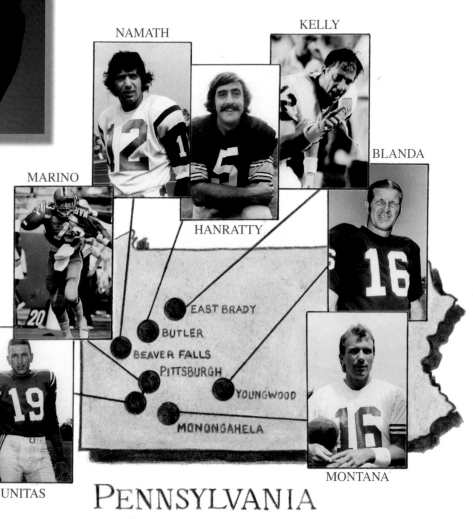

NAMATH

KELLY

MARINO

BLANDA

HANRATTY

EAST BRADY
BUTLER
BEAVER FALLS
PITTSBURGH
YOUNGWOOD
MONONGAHELA

UNITAS

MONTANA

PENNSYLVANIA

I grew up in Pittsburgh, in a section called Oakland. There's my family's old house above. As you can see, the homes were built so close you could stand on your porch and touch the neighbor's house.

In our neighborhood people looked out for each other. They were working-class with a good ethnic mixture—Italian, Irish, African-American, and Polish.

I grew up the oldest child in our close-knit family of five. I have two younger sisters, Cindi and Debbie.

There were no video games or computers when I grew up. There wasn't a lot on TV with just three channels. When I did watch TV as a youngster, my favorite show was "Lassie." Mom says I used to cry when Lassie was in danger.

The families in our neighborhood didn't have extra money to go to movies, pro sports games or vacations. As kids, we spent most of our free time playing outside.

My most traumatic backyard accident happened when I was five. I grabbed a wooden clothesline pole and, as my hand slid down, a hundred stinging slivers pierced my skin.

Mom carefully picked out each one from my trembling hands. Mom always has been there when I needed her.

As I grew, play moved into the street. Jumping on a pogostick was a favorite pastime. I could go anywhere on it. I'd spring up and down our steep stairs.

As you can see from this Christmas morning picture, I loved sports from an early age.

I discovered quickly I had a talent for throwing things. I'd stand and throw balls against our school's brick walls by myself. Other times, I'd run down the street, dodging between parked cars, and throw footballs at targets—telephone poles, trash cans, or stop signs.

I never tried to break anything, although I accidentally shattered about 20 windows at St. Regis, the Catholic grade school across the street from my house. I'd break windows by over-throwing the target or the ball would take a bad hop.

One day, Dad was talking to the pastor at St. Regis when a ball bounced and broke a window 10 feet behind them. They turned to see my embarrassed face.

The sky above Dan's house was often brownish-orange from the nearby steel mills.

My first experience playing football came on our narrow streets. Even though most neighborhood kids were older, I always played quarterback.

It was intimidating at first to play against bigger kids. Those street games helped me develop a mental toughness and love of competition in all sports, including street hockey and baseball.

In the fall, we'd play football in the street after school, stopping every 20 minutes to get out of the way of the city buses that traveled down our street.

The Pittsburgh Steelers were my team. They won four Super Bowls in six years as I grew up. On Sundays, we'd watch the Steelers play on TV and then rush to the street to play our own game during half-time. After the Steelers' game, we'd play until dusk.

When the street light in front of our house clicked on, that was my signal to go home. My parents' rule was we had to be in the house three minutes after the street lights came on. I usually made it home with just seconds to spare.

If I wasn't playing sports in the street, Dad and I often would go up the block to a nearby sports field. Dad drove a newspaper delivery truck at night, so his days were free.

Dad would say, "Do ya wanna go?"

That meant did I want to play catch? I'd always say, "Yeah, sure."

We'd play catch with a football or baseball, depending on the season.

Dad coached a community sandlot football team and taught me how to throw with a quick release by playing catch with me on this field pictured above. In the spring and summer, we'd toss around the baseball. He'd also throw batting practice or hit hundreds of grounders and fly balls.

Dad and I spent many wonderful hours on that field, which the city has since renamed Dan Marino Field. My dad's first name is also Dan, so the field honors him, too. I learned the fundamentals of sports and fatherhood on that field. I learned that a dad who spends time with his son also becomes a friend.

I can honestly say my dad is still one of my best friends. Dad's no-nonsense philosophy can be summed up by the way he taught me how to ride a bike.

He took me to a park one day. We started on the running track, but I couldn't figure out how to keep my balance and pedal at the same time.

We walked to a nearby grassy slope, and I hopped on the old rusty-red bike. Dad pointed me downhill.

"Don't worry about pedaling; just keep your balance," he said.

Then Dad gave me a push. My legs stuck straight out, and I wobbled all the way down before tipping over at the bottom. A couple trips down the hill and I had mastered balance. Then pedaling came easily.

I'm not saying I always liked the push my parents gave me. As I grew older, Dad gave me responsibilities around the house, like taking out the garbage. I'd often put it off, saying, "I'll handle it."

Days would go by and finally Dad would have to yell at me to get it done.

A time my parents were most upset with me happened in sixth grade. I came home from school to find my parents sitting at the kitchen table waiting for me. Mom was crying.

They sat me down and explained that my grades were horrible, and teachers feared I wouldn't make it into high school. That day woke me up. I wasn't dumb; I just didn't give school my best effort.

Some days I'd sit in class watching the clock, not hearing a word the teacher said. All I could think about was getting out of school and playing ball.

My arm got me in trouble one day at our strict Catholic school, taught by nuns. A friend, Dominic DiPaulo, and I started tossing an orange in class while the teacher walked out for a moment. Each throw increased in speed until Dominic threw the orange at me with all his might. I ducked and it hit the wall but it didn't burst. I picked it up and hurled it back at him. Just then, the teacher walked back in the room to see Dominic duck and the orange splatter on the front blackboard. We were both suspended a few days.

In those days, the nuns would smack your hands with wooden rulers for discipline. They rapped my knuckles a few times.

My dreams of playing high school football and beyond are what made me a better student.

In fourth grade, I got my first taste of organized football by being the water boy for the fifth and sixth graders. Here's a picture of me and Billy Sabo, still one of my best friends, after a muddy game on the sidelines.

I wasn't ashamed being the waterboy. We weren't old enough to play. We just loved being around the players. I was also a water boy for Dad's sandlot team, made up of former high school players. I'd go to practices and play catch with them, watch, and dream.

Dad never had the money to take me to Steelers games, but we'd go to high school games all the time.

He'd say, "If you ever want to do this (play in high school), you have to take care of your grades."

After our kitchen-table talk, I realized school and success on and off the field went hand in hand. I needed to pull off my first of many comebacks—this one a classroom comeback.

Dan, left, and Billy Sabo after a muddy day on the sidelines.

Dan and Billy went from waterboys to team leaders at St. Regis. They received team awards in sixth grade. Dan, far right, was the team's Most Valuable Player. Billy, middle, was the defensive MVP. Joey Carcia was the offensive MVP.

Dan (24) with his first football team.

I tried out for football in fifth grade and played quarterback. Our games were Saturday mornings at the same field where Dad and I played catch.

We'd go to church in our uniforms and then walk from the school, up the middle of the street, to the field.

The neighborhood turned out to cheer us, making us all feel special.

The street is also where I learned how to march in a band. I played the bass and snare drums in the school marching band for a couple of years. I marched in a few city parades. As sports took up more time, I picked sports over band. I never stopped loving music, though.

People in our neighborhood probably wished I didn't love music so much. They could hear it blasting from my room.

In junior and senior high I rocked in my room. I loved the hard rock of Ted Nugent. I'd crank up his music and pretend to play the guitar and sing along.

Everyone has secret ambitions; mine was to be a rock singer. I thought I could sing. But when you sing in the shower or with headphones, what sounds good to you doesn't always sound so great to others.

My parents demanded I close all our windows when I acted out my rock dreams.

Several years ago, I met Ted Nugent. I invited him and his son to a Dolphins game and then went to a private concert he performed. My dream of singing did come true—sort of—thanks to my involvement in a charity concert with Hootie & the Blowfish in 1996. They brought me on stage to sing and be in their music video. I sounded terrible, but I had a great time.

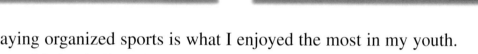

Dan batted over .500 his last two seasons in high school.

He took his driving test after a game was rained out, still wearing his baseball uniform.

The Kansas City Royals drafted Dan in the fourth round of the 1979 draft.

Pittsburgh Post-Gazette

Playing organized sports is what I enjoyed the most in my youth. Along with football, I played Little League baseball.

I got hooked on No. 13 after Dad, my Little League coach, gave me the number because nobody else wanted it.

For a time, I thought baseball would be my best sport. I played through high school as a solid-hitting shortstop and fastball pitcher. After losing once as a freshman, I won 25 straight games on the mound for Central Catholic High. We made it to the state championship my senior year before losing.

I was drafted by the Kansas City Royals, and was tempted to sign with them, but I felt going to college would be more valuable than the $35,000 bonus they offered. I sometimes wonder what would have happened if I played professional baseball.

One thing I never wanted to think about in school was being unable to play sports. Two incidents gave me a scare.

One day I was moving a fish tank for a teacher at St. Regis. I accidentally dropped it in the hallway, and a piece of glass sliced my leg. I needed several stitches. Mom didn't think I should play in our football game a few days later, but Dad cut a hole in a piece of foam and taped it over my wound for protection so I could play.

The next incident almost cost me a foot and my football career. I was mowing wet grass on a hill and slipped. My foot slid within inches of the turning blade, which tore off the front end of my tennis shoe. I walked away unharmed and quit that summer job at the end of the day. My foot was worth more to me than $20 a day.

Marlene Karas/*Pittsburgh Post-Gazette*

Central Catholic had a long tradition of winning football games, and my senior year we won the West Penn Conference championship.

We had some great wins during my days in high school, but two losses stand out in my memory—one of my first junior-varsity games and my last varsity contest.

After spending a productive year on the freshman team, I thought I was ready for the varsity. Then I threw 19 passes without a completion in a junior-varsity game. That kept me humble.

In my last high school game, we played eventual state champion Penn Hills in front of 15,000 fans. They had an overpowering front line that pressured us all game. I completed just 6 of 18 passes with three interceptions in a 14–0 loss. Still, I felt it was one of my best high school performances because they were so tough. Penn Hills finished ranked No. 1 in the country.

Dan was named to the *Parade* magazine High School All-America team after throwing for 1,596 yards and 16 TDs his senior year. Back then, Dan could run—he gained 419 yards. He handled the team's kicking, making 24 of 26 extra points and three field goals and punting 40 yards on average. He is the only player in school history to have his jersey number retired.

Deciding where to play college football was one of the toughest decisions of my life. I gave UCLA, Arizona State, Clemson, Michigan State, and Notre Dame consideration.

In the end, I could see my future from our high school practice field. Behind the city school a tower rises above the surrounding buildings. It's called the Cathedral of Learning, which is the library on the University of Pittsburgh campus. Seeing that tower every day inspired me to work hard on the practice field and in the classroom.

Knowing Dad worked as a landscaper on weekends and Mom earned money as a school crossing guard to send us to Catholic schools also motivated me. I finished high school with a B grade-point average.

I always had the big dream of playing professional football, but I knew I had to go up one step at a time.

People say my quick steps in the pocket have helped my career. I believe my quick feet come from skipping rope. In high school, I'd skip rope all the time to stay in shape. I'd even skip rope down the street while going to a friend's house or running an errand.

Anthony Neste

Ed Morgan/*Pittsburgh Post-Gazette*

Despite all the positive points of other schools, nothing could match staying close to home. I chose the University of Pittsburgh, which is just four blocks from my house.

Staying home allowed family and friends to see more of my games. I also wanted to support my sisters. I always have had a strong bond with them.

Cindi enjoyed sports and drama. I'd go to her games, and bring her flowers at her stage performances. Sometimes I'd let her tag along when I went out with friends.

Debbie had her own special talents, more artistic than athletic, and she was somewhat shy. I remember a day she cut her head in elementary school and needed stitches at the emergency room. Word reached me that she wanted me there because I had experience with stitches. I met her at the hospital and held her hand while doctors closed the wound.

Dan with tight end Benjie Pryor before the Fiesta Bowl.

I suffered my share of wounds playing at Pitt. Having family nearby helped me through rough times.

My college career started with a splash. An injury to the number-one quarterback thrust me into the starting role the seventh game of my freshman season. I completed my first college pass on my 18th birthday. We won five straight with me at quarterback to finish 11–1, ranked seventh in the country.

My hot start cooled in my sophomore year when a knee injury shortened my season. I watched as our team went 11–1 again and finished second in the polls.

Football expectations were high going into my junior year in 1981. People compared me to Johnny Unitas and predicted I'd win the Heisman Trophy, presented to college football's top player.

Everything went as planned until our home game against rival Penn State. We came in undefeated and top ranked in the nation. The whole city buzzed.

But Penn State demolished us, 48–14, ending our dreams of a national championship.

After that game, I started hearing hometown fans bad-mouth my play for the first time. People trashed me on the local call-in radio shows and in the newspapers.

Winning and praise make life easy. The true test of character is how you handle losing and criticism.

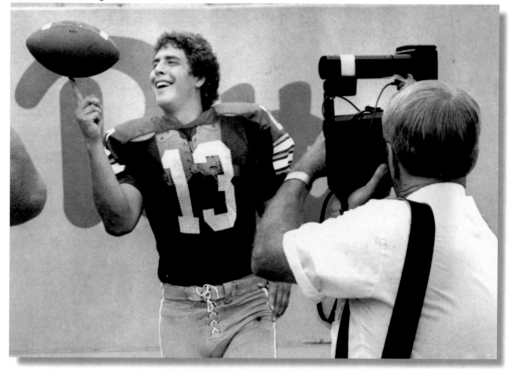

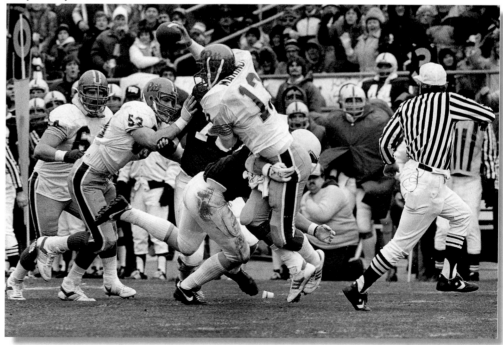

While others tried to bring me down, Dad built me up.

I went home for dinner a couple of times a week and usually brought some teammates. I'd see Dad in the stands at practice and hold up a finger count of how many guys I planned to bring home that night. But my busy college schedule didn't allow much time to talk with Dad one-on-one. So Dad wrote me letters.

The letters were always positive and filled with advice and sayings I could carry with me. When people started criticizing me, he'd write: "You have to rise above it."

Those letters meant the world to me, knowing Dad always believed in me. I saved all those letters and have them in a shoe box at my home today.

Despite the disappointing Penn State loss, the season ended with a thrilling Sugar Bowl victory against Georgia.

Down 20–17 with 3:46 left, we drove 80 yards for the victory, capped by my 33–yard touchdown pass to John Brown with 35 seconds to play.

The excitement at Pitt wore off my senior year as a coaching change and an underachieving 9–3 season brought back the boos. I finished my college career with a 7–3 loss to Southern Methodist in the Cotton Bowl.

Sports, and life, are like a roller-coaster ride. You have to take the ups with the downs. All the criticism and struggles my senior year made me mentally tougher in the long run. Looking back, the season prepared me more for the NFL than if I had won the Heisman Trophy.

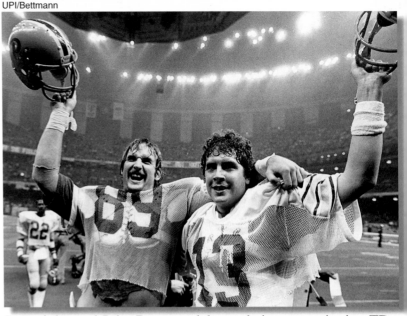

Dan, right, and John Brown celebrate their game-winning TD.

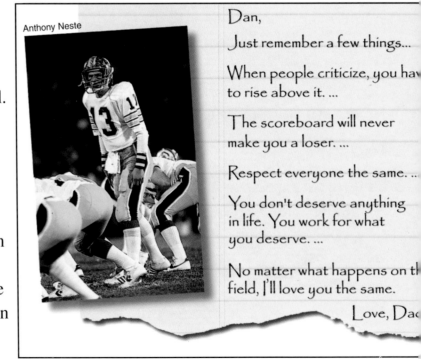

Dan,

Just remember a few things...

When people criticize, you hav to rise above it. ...

The scoreboard will never make you a loser. ...

Respect everyone the same. ...

You don't deserve anything in life. You work for what you deserve. ...

No matter what happens on th field, I'll love you the same.

Love, Dac

Dan left Pitt as the Panthers all-time leading passer, with nine school records, including career yards (8,597) and touchdowns (79). The Panthers were 38–3 with Dan as the starting quarterback. He made the All-America team as a junior. Pitt has retired his football jersey number.

1983 NFL Draft

1. **John Elway**
2. Eric Dickerson
3. Curt Warner
4. Chris Hinton
5. Billy Ray Smith
6. Jimbo Covert
7. **Todd Blackledge**
8. Michael Maddix
9. Bruce Matthews
10. Terry Kinard
11. Tim Lewis
12. Tony Hunter
13. James Jones
14. **Jim Kelly**
15. **Tony Eason**
16. Mike Pitts
17. Leonard Smith
18. Willie Gault
19. Joey Browner
20. Gary Anderson
21. Gabe Rivera
22. Gill Byrd
23. Jim Jeffcoat
24. **Ken O'Brien**
25. Dave Remington
26. Don Mosebar
27. **Dan Marino**
28. Darrell Green

QBs in bold.

Three days after the 1983 Cotton Bowl, the upstart United States Football League drafted me number one.

I was flattered, but playing in the NFL was my ultimate goal, so I waited for its spring draft. Family and friends gathered at our house on draft day.

Farther and farther I slipped as five quarterbacks were taken ahead of me. My heart sank when my beloved Steelers picked lineman Gabe Rivera instead of me.

Finally, on the 27th pick of the first round, the Miami Dolphins announced my name. I made a decision not to be bitter at the teams that passed on me. Instead, I chose to count my blessings and focus my energy on the opportunity at hand.

I graduated from Pitt that spring with a B average and a degree in communications. Not bad, considering my early school problems.

I had confidence in my abilities entering my first Dolphins camp. As a rookie, I had to sing my college fight song in the cafeteria or be dumped in our nearby pond.

Respecting everyone equally helped me find harmony with head coach Don Shula. I respected him for his accomplishments, but I wasn't awed by him.

I think he respected me for that, and we became good friends. I owe much to Coach Shula. He pushed me hard my early years. I studied the game more and developed quicker than if he had gone easy on me. Sometimes we need to be pushed to improve.

I didn't think I would start right away for the Dolphins, but I felt I would get my chance early. The year before, the Dolphins had the NFL's worst passing rating despite making it to the Super Bowl.

My chance to start came in the sixth week against the Buffalo Bills. We were down 14–0, but came back to force the game into overtime before losing. I threw for 322 yards and three touchdowns. Although we lost, we all felt a new passing era in Miami had begun.

A knee sprain kept me out of the last two regular-season games. I made it back in time for the playoffs, only to lose to Seattle.

I learned a lot that first season and was honored to play in the Pro Bowl with the NFL's greatest players.

Dan posted the greatest rookie quarterback season ever, leading the AFC with a 96 passing rating, including 2,210 yards, 20 TDs and just 6 interceptions. He was the first rookie QB to start in the Pro Bowl.

The success of my first season made me hungrier to improve.

The 1984 season was simply magical—a year in which the skills of everyone came together. We started 11–0, drawing comparisons to Shula's undefeated 1972 Dolphins. That talk ended a week later with our overtime loss to San Diego.

The defeat proved a temporary setback as we cruised through the playoffs, including a sweet home victory over Pittsburgh, for a Super Bowl showdown with the once-beaten San Francisco 49ers and quarterback Joe Montana.

Because of our team's record-setting passing numbers and Montana's history of big-game wins, much of the attention focused on Joe and myself. We even did a soft drink commercial together before the game, with Joe buying me a pop. I then offered to buy the next one, which meant people expected our Super Bowl showdown to be the first of many clashes.

It didn't work out that way.

Our game plan didn't go as expected either.

We scored on our first two possessions, but the 49ers' defense tightened and their offense played flawlessly. The 49ers won 38–16.

Maybe we were satisfied just to be in the Super Bowl. I know I tried my hardest, but I know I could have played better. We all could have.

Sitting in the locker room and experiencing the crush of a Super Bowl loss remains my biggest disappointment.

Surviving that setback, however, has been a victory. No matter how big the fall, you can always get up. I've also learned what happens on the field should stay on the field.

Ten days after the Super Bowl, I married my college sweetheart, Claire Veazey, in St. Regis Church, the same church across from my parents' house. Our Super Bowl loss didn't spoil the wedding one bit.

The whole neighborhood turned out and wished us well on our special day. Claire has been my partner in life since then, and we've been through a lot together. I'm lucky to be with her.

Thinking we'd get right back to the Super Bowl softened the 49ers loss for me and my teammates.

The next 11 seasons, however, we made the playoffs only five times and never made it back to the Super Bowl. Some years our defense faltered, others our offense struggled as I made my share of mistakes, too.

Through the struggle I tried to stay positive and keep doing what I do best—throwing the football. To keep going when there is no end in sight takes faith.

Marc Serota

AP/Wide World Photos

Winning a Super Bowl takes the right group of people and a little fate. Sometimes the hardest workers and the best teams don't win. That's what makes sports interesting. At times it all doesn't seem fair. But guess what? Life's not fair.

I started a record 145 games in a row, despite five off-season knee operations, until a freak Achilles injury forced me to miss most of the 1993 season.

Sitting out made me appreciate that playing sports is a day-by-day privilege, not a right.

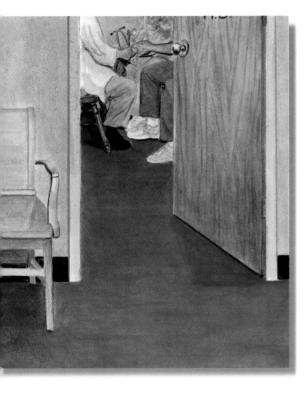

In the same way, I didn't understand the privilege of being a parent until a problem arose in my family.

Claire and I have four children—Daniel, Michael, Joseph, and Alexandria. Each has their own special talents.

Michael, however, was born with a mild form of autism. We discovered it when he was about 2½ years old.

The mysterious disorder mixes up signals in the brain, and in some cases, causes children to withdraw from the world around them.

Of course we wanted answers to why this happened. Sometimes, though, we never understand why. My lifelong philosophy always has been to accept the situation you're in without blame, then do your best to improve it. In Michael's case, we focused on improving his life.

With help, Michael is making great strides. To me, Michael has more courage than anyone I've known. At times, just to play in the game of life takes the greatest courage of all.

Michael's comeback has been an inspiration to me and helped me return to football after my injury.

After tearing the Achilles tendon in the back of my heel, I realized I needed to take care of my body better. I worked out harder in the offseason and did more stretching.

My first game back proved memorable because we rallied from behind in the last minute to beat New England 39–35.

During my career as a starter, so far, the Dolphins have won 32 games after trailing in the fourth quarter. Leading a comeback is one of the best feelings in sports.

People ask how I stay focused under pressure.

Marc Serota

Like everyone, fear of failure is a motivator. Before a game I always feel nervous. During the game, however, I never think about failure.

I never think: "What's going to happen if I miss this throw?" If I worried about making mistakes, I probably would throw an incompletion or interception.

During a game, the only thoughts I have are positive. I always say, "If there's time on the clock, then we're still in the game."

One of the Dolphins' greatest comebacks came in 1994 while on the New York Jets' home field.

We trailed by 22 points in the first half and it seemed the whole world was against us. Slowly, we battled back. With 30 seconds to play, we had a first-and-goal at the Jets' eight with no timeouts, down by three points.

Everyone expected us to stop the clock by me spiking the ball to the ground. Instead, we did the unexpected. We called it the "clock" play.

I faked the spike and tossed it to Mark Ingram for the game-winning touchdown, stunning the Jets and their fans.

Silencing your critics with unexpected success is an awesome feeling.

Jan. 4, 1986: Miami 24, Cleveland 21
Completes four of six passes for 60 yards in fourth quarter.

Jan. 5, 1991: Miami 17, Kansas City 16
Scores twice in final quarter on 8-for-8 passing with 101 yards.

Sept. 14, 1992: Miami 27, Cleveland 23
Drives 84 yards in 68 seconds for TD with 7 seconds left.

Sept. 4, 1994: Miami 39, N. England 35
Audibles on fourth-and-five to throw 35-yard TD for winning score.

Nov. 27, 1994: Miami 28, NY Jets 24
"Clock" play completes 18-point, third-quarter comeback.

Life sometimes throws you unexpected surprises you just have to grab. For me, one came when a movie producer asked me to appear in a film about a pet detective who rescues a kidnapped Super Bowl quarterback.

After talking it over with my agent, Ralph Stringer, we decided to pass. But the producers were persistent.

They kept calling. Then they told me some guy named Jim Carrey would be in it. I'd never heard of him.

Finally, the producers convinced us to meet them and Jim at a restaurant in Los Angeles. Again we told them, "Thanks, but no thanks."

Carrey wouldn't take no for an answer. Before we could leave, he started doing scenes from the movie right there. He blurted out hilarious one-liners and flopped around on the floor. He cracked me up, and everyone in the restaurant stopped eating to listen and laugh.

Ralph and I finally decided my part in *Ace Ventura: Pet Detective* was simply about making fun of myself. We agreed to do the movie. I'm glad I did.

I learned a lot about how movies are made and gained a new respect for how hard actors and film crews work.

Some of my best memories during the filming came during the breaks. As soon as the director said "Cut!" to end filming, some from the crew would drop everything and take off running for a pass.

I'd grab footballs and start firing passes over and through the equipment.

Those guys made some of the best diving catches I've ever seen. I don't know who enjoyed it more, them or me.

When the zany movie came out, I thought it turned out great and was pleasantly surprised by its success.

I didn't win any awards for my acting debut, but at least I tried. There's no embarrassment in trying new things, even if you're not the best.

My most embarrassing sports moments have come on the golf course. I love the game and at times can score well. I'm as competitive on the golf course as I am on the football field.

But as all golfers, I've hit my share of terrible shots, some while playing in celebrity tournaments. I've hit onlookers with the golf ball a few times. Fortunately, no one has been seriously hurt.

One time during a televised tournament with lots of people watching, I missed an important putt from one foot away. Deep inside I wanted to scream and throw that putter as far as I could. Thankfully, I didn't and kept my cool.

Marc Serota

Tom DiPace

Another thing I'm thankful for is the opportunity to be involved in special charity work. Football is important, but it's street play compared with the problems and suffering many people face each day.

My wife and I started the Dan Marino Foundation in 1992. I'm proud of the fact it has raised more than $2 million for the youth of South Florida.

I've worked with many charities over the years that do important work. Some of my most memorable experiences, however, have come from working with the Make-A-Wish Foundation. They grant wishes for kids who are dying. Children have asked to meet me, and other Dolphin players, from time to time.

I try to lift their spirits any way I can. When they leave, however, it's tough because the sadness of their situation breaks me up inside. I'll always remember meeting a young boy from Pittsburgh in 1994. His last wish was to meet me, so I met him and his family on Christmas Day. After spending time together, he gave me a pin shaped like an angel. He said, "When I'm not around anymore, I'm gonna be watching over you."

Man, I didn't know what to say, other than "thanks" through my tears.

Meeting Make-A-Wish children has shown me the power of encouragement, which we all have, and a secret: When you give of yourself, you become a receiver, too.

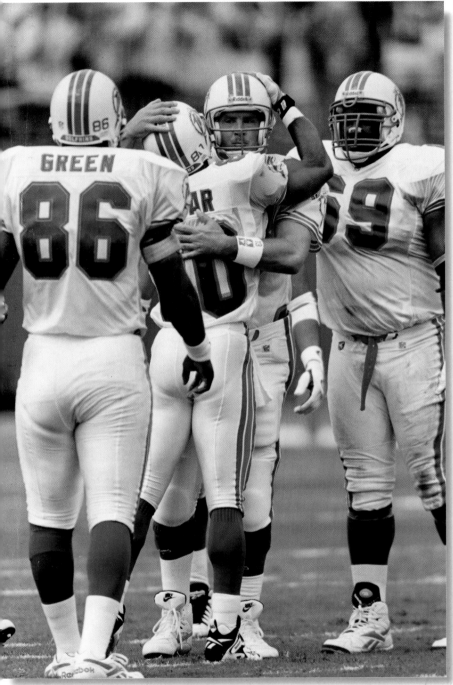

One of my proudest moments on the football field came during the 1995 season. That year I set several NFL career passing records. Most meaningful was throwing my 343rd touchdown pass, breaking Fran Tarkenton's old mark.

Having my parents and my family at the game to share the moment made it special. Tarkenton was there, too, and graciously congratulated me. Someday maybe I'll be in the stands when someone breaks my records.

I'm honored by the recognition of my records, but my goals have never been to pass for a certain number of touchdowns or yards. If you focus on personal records, that could hurt your team's chances of winning.

Winning a Super Bowl always has been my ultimate dream in the NFL.

I haven't lived that yet. Maybe I'll get another Super Bowl chance thanks to the new enthusiasm coach Jimmy Johnson has brought to the Dolphins.

If it doesn't happen, there will be a little hole inside me, but I'll survive. I've been part of many big wins. Lack of a Super Bowl ring won't take anything away from my career.

In the end, being first and achieving all your goals doesn't happen all the time.

Still, I think you should dream big dreams, as long as you're willing to work toward those dreams. Never look back and say, "If only I had done this or that, I could have reached my dreams."

When you have a dream, your first and only goal should be to prepare yourself as best you can and try your best. That's all anyone can ask. When you do that, as my dad says, no matter what the scoreboard reads, you'll always walk away a winner.